Mel Robbin's Let Them Theory

How Letting Go of What You Can't Control Can Transform Your Life

By

Rob Walker

Contents

Introduction

The Power of Two Words: Let Them

Imagine a life where you no longer feel weighed down by the opinions of others. A life where you can stop endlessly comparing yourself to your colleagues, friends, or strangers on social media. Picture being free from the constant pressure to manage every detail of your life, from your career to your relationships. What would that life look like?

The answer lies in two simple, yet profoundly powerful words: **Let Them**.

"Let Them" is a concept that's simple to say but often difficult to put into practice. These two words represent the art of relinquishing control over things that are out of your hands—people's judgments, expectations, and the need to constantly seek external validation. This book is about helping you unlock the power of **Let Them**, so you can focus on the one thing you have control over: **yourself**.

When we're trapped in the cycle of trying to please others or worrying about what they think, we drain ourselves of energy and lose sight of what truly matters. But when you say, "Let Them," you're freeing yourself from the chaos of external expectations and putting your energy where it belongs—on your own happiness, your own goals, and your own peace of mind.

Why We Struggle with Control and External Validation

Have you ever found yourself caught in a web of trying to control everything and everyone around you? Maybe it's been about managing your boss's expectations, your friends' feelings, or your family's demands. Or perhaps, you've spent hours obsessing over how others perceive you—worried about what they'll think if you fail or succeed, if you speak up or stay silent. This is a natural response in a world that constantly tells us to measure our worth by what others think or do.

We are wired, both biologically and culturally, to seek validation. From an evolutionary perspective, being accepted by the group was essential for survival. Our brains are designed to avoid conflict and seek approval, and that often means sacrificing our own desires and authenticity to fit in. Over time, this instinct can grow into a toxic need for external validation—be it in the form of likes on social media, praise from a boss, or approval from friends and family.

The problem arises when we give too much power to these external sources. We start making decisions based on what we think others want, rather than what we truly need or desire. We end up feeling overwhelmed, anxious, and, at times, like we're living someone else's life.

The Let Them Theory offers an antidote to this constant struggle. It teaches us to acknowledge our instincts and desires, but then choose to release control over things outside our sphere of influence. We can't control how others feel, think, or react—but we can control how much we let it affect us.

How This Book Will Change Your Life

Now, imagine a life where you stop putting so much energy into managing the uncontrollable. A life where you take back the power that's been drained by seeking external approval and worrying about everyone else's opinion. **The Let Them Theory** is about teaching you exactly how to do that.

In the pages ahead, you'll learn:

- **Why you've been spending so much time and energy trying to control things outside of your control**, and how this is preventing you from achieving your goals and finding happiness.
- **How to release the grip of others' expectations**, so you can start focusing on what truly matters to you: your happiness, your dreams, your life.
- **The science behind letting go**—why our brains are wired to seek validation and how we can retrain them to prioritize our own well-being and self-worth.

- **Practical tools and techniques** for applying the Let Them philosophy in every area of your life, from relationships to career, and even your personal growth.
- **Real-life stories and examples** of how others have used this philosophy to transform their lives, reduce stress, and reclaim their personal power.

By the end of this book, you will have the tools and mindset to stop wasting time on the wrong things and start putting your energy into the only thing you can control: **yourself**.

Imagine the freedom of waking up every day, knowing that the weight of others' opinions, judgments, and expectations no longer dictates your actions. Picture the energy you'll free up to focus on the goals that truly matter to you—whether that's building a career you love, cultivating meaningful relationships, or simply finding peace in your own skin.

This is not just about making changes in how you think; it's about empowering you to take action in your own life. The Let Them Theory is a call to arms for anyone who's tired of living in the shadows of others' expectations and is ready to step into their own power.

Welcome to the journey of taking your life back. The Let Them Theory is the key that unlocks the door to a life of freedom, joy, and fulfillment. The power to change is already within you—and it all starts with two words: **Let Them**.

Reclaiming Your Power

Understanding the Let Them Theory

The foundation of *The Let Them Theory* is both simple and profound: we can only control ourselves, not others. The sooner we realize this truth, the sooner we can stop wasting our energy on the things we cannot change and start focusing on what truly matters—our own well-being, growth, and happiness.

The phrase "Let Them" is an invitation to release the burden of trying to control other people, their opinions, or their behavior. It's a challenge to stop obsessing over the judgments and expectations of others, which so often lead us into a cycle of frustration, self-doubt, and burnout. In its simplest form, *The Let Them Theory* says: "Let them be who they are, and let yourself be who you are."

When you choose to "Let Them," you give yourself permission to stop managing the uncontrollable. Instead of trying to predict what others will think or how they will react, you can focus your energy on making decisions that align with your values and desires. You create space to be authentically yourself, without constantly adjusting or bending to fit someone else's mold.

This is not about becoming indifferent or disconnected from people—it's about empowering yourself by realizing that other people's opinions and behaviors are outside your control. *The Let Them Theory* teaches us that we can still care for others, support them, and build meaningful relationships, but we no longer need to center our lives around their approval.

The Hidden Costs of Trying to Control Everything

Let's be honest: we all have an instinct to control. It's a survival mechanism that has been ingrained in us for centuries. At work, we want to control our outcomes—our boss's opinion, our team's performance, the trajectory of our career. In relationships, we want to control how others feel about us—our partner's affection, our friend's loyalty, the approval of our parents. But the more we try to control, the more we end up feeling exhausted, overwhelmed, and powerless.

The hidden cost of this behavior is often invisible at first—it sneaks up on us over time. But when we give too much of our energy to managing others, it starts to eat away at our well-being in ways that are hard to ignore.

Here are some of the most common costs we pay when we try to control everything:

1. **Mental and Emotional Exhaustion**: Constantly worrying about other people's feelings and reactions takes a huge toll on your mental health. You may feel drained by the effort of keeping up appearances or adjusting your behavior to suit different people and situations. This emotional labor is taxing and unsustainable in the long run.

2. **Loss of Self-Identity**: When you are always adjusting your actions to gain approval or avoid conflict, you lose touch with who you truly are. You become so focused on fulfilling other people's needs and expectations that you forget what makes you unique, what you truly want, and what drives you. Over time, this can lead to a sense of disconnection and confusion about your own desires.

3. **Strained Relationships**: Trying to control other people often leads to resentment—either from you or from them. When you try to "fix" someone or manipulate their reactions, it damages trust and emotional intimacy. Healthy relationships are built on mutual respect, not on one person trying to control the other.

4. **Missed Opportunities**: The more you try to predict and control outcomes, the more you limit yourself. You may avoid taking risks, making mistakes, or stepping out of your comfort zone because you're

afraid of what others will think. This fear of judgment and failure can prevent you from reaching your full potential, both personally and professionally.

5. **Chronic Stress**: Trying to manage everything and everyone around you generates a constant low-level anxiety that's hard to shake off. The stress of needing to be "perfect" or in control at all times can lead to burnout, physical health problems, and an overall sense of dissatisfaction with life.

How Releasing Control Leads to Freedom

Releasing control may seem counterintuitive at first. How can letting go of control lead to more freedom? Won't we just lose direction or become passive? The truth is that it's quite the opposite. When you let go of the things you can't control, you make space for what you *can* control—your thoughts, your actions, your mindset, and your response to life's challenges.

Here's how releasing control leads to freedom:

1. **Freedom from External Expectations**: The moment you decide to "Let Them"—whether it's a judgmental colleague, an overbearing relative, or societal pressures—you release the burden of needing to meet their expectations. Instead, you

define your own path, based on your core values, desires, and aspirations. No longer bound by the opinions of others, you can take bold steps toward living a life that truly reflects who you are.

2. **Freedom to Focus on What Truly Matters**: When you stop investing energy in trying to manage other people, you redirect that energy toward the things that matter most to you. You can prioritize your goals, nurture your relationships, and pursue your dreams without being constantly distracted by external demands. You can finally give your full attention to the areas of your life that deserve it most.

3. **Freedom to Make Authentic Choices**: By letting go of the need for approval or control, you're free to make decisions that reflect your authentic self. You don't have to constantly second-guess yourself or worry about how others will react. This leads to greater confidence, inner peace, and a sense of alignment with your true self.

4. **Freedom to Embrace Imperfection**: Releasing control doesn't mean you abandon responsibility—it means embracing the uncertainty and imperfections of life. You stop trying to micromanage every outcome and instead start trusting the process. You give yourself permission

to fail, learn, and grow without the fear of judgment or failure weighing you down.

5. **Freedom to Experience True Connection**: Ironically, when you let go of the need to control others, you open the door to deeper, more authentic connections. People are drawn to those who are genuine and unafraid to be themselves. By freeing yourself from expectations, you invite others to do the same, creating space for more honest, fulfilling relationships.

Reclaiming your power through *The Let Them Theory* isn't about becoming indifferent or selfish—it's about recognizing that your power lies in how you respond to the world, not in controlling it. By letting go of the things you can't control, you free yourself to live a life of true meaning, authenticity, and joy.

In the following chapters, we'll dive deeper into how you can apply this theory to every area of your life—from work to relationships to personal growth. You'll discover the practical steps you can take to stop wasting energy on things that drain you, and start focusing on the things that will truly bring you fulfillment and success.

The Science of Letting Go

How Our Brains Are Wired for Validation

From the moment we're born, our brains are hardwired to seek connection and approval from others. This instinct is deeply rooted in our evolutionary biology, where being accepted by the group was crucial for survival. Early humans depended on their social groups for protection, food, and resources, and being rejected by the group could mean isolation, vulnerability, and even death. Because of this, our brains developed a powerful drive to seek approval, avoid judgment, and fit in.

In modern society, this same primal drive to belong manifests as our need for **validation**—the feeling that we are seen, valued, and accepted by others. Whether it's praise at work, likes on social media, or approval from friends and family, validation reinforces our sense of self-worth and identity. But while this instinct was once essential for survival, it has evolved into a double-edged sword in the modern world.

Today, the need for external validation can become a trap. We often tie our self-worth to the opinions and approval of others, leading to a cycle of dependence on external feedback. This need for validation can cloud our judgment, make us overly concerned with how others perceive us, and prevent us from being authentic.

When we seek constant validation, we give away our personal power. We start living for others—choosing career paths, relationships, and lifestyles based on the approval we expect to receive rather than what genuinely fulfills us. **The Let Them Theory** challenges this deep-seated need for validation by urging us to reclaim our inner sense of worth, separate from others' opinions.

The Neuroscience of Control and Freedom

The way our brains process control and freedom is not just psychological—it's neurological. Understanding the neuroscience behind these concepts can give us a deeper appreciation of why letting go of control is so liberating.

When we try to control external factors—whether it's how others perceive us or the outcomes of situations—we activate specific areas of the brain involved in **cognitive control**. These areas, such as the prefrontal cortex, are responsible for executive functions like planning, decision-making, and regulating our responses. In many ways, trying to control things outside of our influence is exhausting because it demands continuous, high-level cognitive energy.

However, studies in neuroscience show that **perceived control** can be beneficial, but only up to a point. In fact, excessive control can actually lead to heightened stress and anxiety. When we can't control outcomes, the brain experiences a **fear response**, which triggers the fight-or-flight mechanism. This is why we feel anxious, restless, or overwhelmed when trying to manage situations beyond our ability to influence.

On the flip side, **letting go** of the need to control can shift the brain's response to a state of relaxation and clarity. When we accept that we cannot control everything, the brain moves out of the fight-or-flight mode and into a **parasympathetic** state, which is the "rest and digest" mode. This allows us to experience feelings of calmness, reduced stress, and greater cognitive clarity.

The **release of control** is also linked to higher levels of **dopamine**, the brain's reward neurotransmitter. When we stop trying to control the uncontrollable, the brain rewards us with a sense of relief and contentment. We also begin to experience greater creativity, as the mind is freed from constant worry and can focus on more constructive, purposeful thinking.

In short, neuroscience tells us that when we relinquish the need for external control, we can achieve a **greater sense of well-being**, reduced anxiety, and a more peaceful, focused state of mind. The act of letting go becomes a powerful tool not just for mental health, but for overall brain function and productivity.

Research-Backed Reasons to Stop Worrying About What You Can't Control

A wealth of psychological and neuroscientific research supports the idea that letting go of the things you cannot control is a critical step toward a more fulfilling and stress-free life. The evidence clearly shows that trying to control things outside our sphere of influence is not only futile, but it also undermines our mental and physical health.

Here are several key research-backed reasons why you should stop worrying about what you can't control:

1. **The Illusion of Control Leads to Anxiety** A study published in the *Journal of Personality and Social Psychology* found that people who try to control situations that are inherently uncontrollable experience higher levels of anxiety and stress. When you believe that you can control something that's beyond your power (like other people's opinions or the outcome of a situation), the brain perceives this as a threat. The constant tension of trying to "manage" these uncontrollable factors leads to chronic anxiety.

2. **Letting Go Increases Happiness and Well-being**
   Research from the *University of California, Berkeley* showed that individuals who practiced mindfulness and acceptance (which are key components of letting go) reported higher levels of happiness and lower levels of stress. These studies suggest that releasing the need to control everything allows us to cultivate a sense of peace and contentment, which enhances our emotional well-being.

3. **The Power of Acceptance**
   The concept of **Radical Acceptance**, as outlined in the work of psychologist Tara Brach, is grounded in the idea that accepting reality as it is—without trying to change it—can lead to profound emotional healing. Research shows that accepting what we cannot control fosters **resilience**, making us better equipped to handle life's challenges without becoming overwhelmed by them.

4. **Focus on What You Can Control for Better Health**
   A study published in the *Journal of Behavioral Medicine* found that focusing on things within your control—such as your own thoughts, behaviors, and actions—can reduce stress and improve health outcomes. By letting go of the need to control others, you free up mental and physical resources to focus on your own well-being, which in turn

improves both your psychological health and your immune system.

5. **Letting Go Leads to More Productive Thinking** According to research in the *Journal of Experimental Social Psychology*, trying to control uncontrollable factors can lead to "cognitive overload," a state where our brains are so bogged down by worry that we lose our ability to think clearly and make decisions. When we let go of control, we allow ourselves to think more creatively and approach problems with a fresh perspective.

6. **Improved Relationships with Others** Studies show that when we release control over how others act or think, we open up space for more genuine and authentic relationships. A study from *Stanford University* found that people who let go of trying to control their partner's behavior experience more satisfaction in relationships. This is because both people feel free to be themselves, rather than constantly trying to meet the other's expectations.

Letting Go of Other People's Opinions

Breaking Free from the Prison of Approval-Seeking

We've all been there: constantly checking for approval, waiting for a "thumbs up" or a compliment to feel validated. It's a cycle that seems innocent at first—just a harmless desire to be liked or accepted. But over time, the need for approval can become a prison, limiting our freedom and preventing us from fully embracing who we are.

This prison of approval-seeking is built on the belief that our self-worth is dependent on what others think of us. The more we seek approval, the more power we give to others over our happiness and sense of identity. We adjust our behavior, opinions, and even our values based on what we think will get us the most positive feedback.

The problem is that **approval-seeking** is an exhausting and unsustainable strategy. It creates a constant cycle of striving for external validation and never feeling truly satisfied. Whether it's from a boss, a partner, a friend, or even strangers on social media, relying on others' opinions to define who we are will always leave us vulnerable to uncertainty and rejection.

To break free from this cycle, we must realize that we don't need others' approval to be enough. We are inherently valuable, regardless of how others see us. When we make the shift from seeking validation externally to validating ourselves internally, we step out of the prison of approval-seeking and into the freedom of self-empowerment.

The Toxic Effects of Comparison and Judgment

We live in a world that constantly encourages comparison. Social media platforms are designed to highlight the best versions of people's lives, careers, and bodies, creating a never-ending stream of images to compare ourselves to. Whether it's a colleague's promotion, a friend's vacation, or someone's fitness transformation, the act of comparing ourselves to others has become an ingrained part of modern life.

Comparison may seem harmless, but it's one of the most insidious ways we can undermine our own sense of self-worth. Research has shown that **upward comparison**—comparing ourselves to those we perceive as doing better than us—can lead to feelings of inadequacy, jealousy, and anxiety. It's a natural human instinct to compare, but it's also a powerful source of unhappiness.

The **toxic effects of comparison** are not limited to how we feel about our accomplishments. They also extend to how we judge others. When we judge others, we reinforce the belief that our own worth is tied to others' actions and choices. This leads to a judgmental mindset, where we're constantly sizing people up and measuring them against an arbitrary standard of success or attractiveness. This only perpetuates the cycle of seeking validation through comparison.

The antidote to this toxic comparison is **self-acceptance**—the ability to embrace our own uniqueness without measuring ourselves against anyone else. Instead of looking outward for validation, we need to look inward, focusing on what we're doing well and celebrating our own progress.

How to Build Your Own Self-Validation System

The key to breaking free from the prison of approval-seeking and escaping the toxic effects of comparison is to build your own **self-validation system**. This means shifting the source of your worth and self-esteem from external validation (what others think of you) to internal validation (how you think about yourself).

Building a self-validation system isn't about becoming arrogant or dismissive of others. It's about **recognizing that you are enough just as you are**, without needing to rely on others' approval. Here are several steps to help you create a strong self-validation system:

1. **Understand Your Core Values** Self-validation begins with understanding what matters most to you. What are your core values? What do you stand for? When you are clear on your values, it becomes easier to validate your own decisions and actions because they align with what's most important to you. Instead of seeking approval from others, you'll feel confident in your choices because they are rooted in your authentic self.

2. **Celebrate Your Small Wins** One of the most powerful ways to build self-validation is to acknowledge and celebrate your own accomplishments—no matter how small. Whether it's completing a project at work, making progress in your personal goals, or simply getting through a challenging day, recognizing your successes reinforces your self-worth. Make it a habit to celebrate your progress rather than waiting for someone else to notice or praise you.

3. **Shift Your Focus to Internal Growth** Instead of measuring your success based on others' achievements, focus on your own personal growth. How have you improved over time? What new skills have you developed? What challenges have you overcome? By focusing on your own journey, rather than comparing it to others' paths, you can

start to validate yourself based on the progress you're making—not on external benchmarks.

4. **Practice Self-Compassion** Self-compassion is essential to building self-validation. When you make mistakes or fall short of your own expectations, instead of criticizing yourself or seeking validation from others, practice kindness and understanding. Treat yourself the way you would treat a close friend—encouraging, supportive, and patient. This shift in mindset allows you to validate your worth even in the face of failure or imperfection.

5. **Learn to Set Boundaries** Part of self-validation is protecting your energy and time by setting clear boundaries. When you stop seeking constant approval from others, you can establish limits on how much you allow others' opinions to influence your decisions. Boundaries help preserve your self-worth by ensuring that your choices align with your values, not with what others expect of you.

6. **Cultivate a Growth Mindset** A growth mindset is the belief that abilities and intelligence can be developed through hard work, dedication, and learning. Instead of seeking validation based on where you are now, focus on your potential for growth. Every challenge is an

opportunity to improve, and every setback is a chance to learn. By embracing a growth mindset, you can validate yourself based on your effort and progress, rather than comparing yourself to others.

The Freedom to Be You

Stop Living for Others, Start Living for Yourself

For most of us, it's easy to fall into the trap of living for others. From childhood to adulthood, we're taught to seek approval from our parents, teachers, friends, bosses, and society. We adjust our behavior, choices, and goals to meet others' expectations, all in the hope of being accepted, loved, and valued. Over time, this habit becomes ingrained, and we begin to lose sight of what we truly want in life.

Living for others can feel like an act of kindness or responsibility at first, but in reality, it can drain us emotionally and spiritually. We become disconnected from our own desires, needs, and values. We begin to prioritize pleasing others over our own well-being, and in doing so, we sacrifice our personal happiness and authenticity.

The freedom to be truly yourself lies in the moment you stop living for others and start living for yourself. It's about making decisions based on your values, goals, and what feels right for you, not on the expectations or judgments of others. This doesn't mean you should be selfish or disregard the feelings of others—it means you're taking ownership of your own life and making choices that align with your true self.

When you begin to prioritize your own happiness and authenticity, you stop being a passive participant in your own life. You take the reins, knowing that your worth is not determined by the opinions or approval of anyone else. The freedom to be you is about giving yourself permission to live fully, to make mistakes, to take risks, and to grow into the person you were meant to be.

Identifying Your Core Values and Desires

The first step toward living for yourself is understanding who you truly are and what matters most to you. This starts with **identifying your core values**—the principles and beliefs that guide your decisions and actions. Your core values are the compass that helps you navigate through life and make choices that align with your authentic self.

To begin identifying your core values, ask yourself questions like:

- What principles do I want to live by?
- What qualities do I admire in others?
- When have I felt the most fulfilled or at peace with myself?

- What causes or issues am I deeply passionate about?

By reflecting on these questions, you can start to uncover the values that drive you. These could be things like **honesty**, **freedom**, **family**, **creativity**, **growth**, **justice**, or **compassion**. Your values are deeply personal and unique to you—no one else can define them for you.

Once you've identified your core values, it becomes much easier to understand what you truly desire in life. Desire is often tangled with external expectations or social conditioning, but when you reconnect with your values, you begin to see your desires more clearly.

Ask yourself:

- What do I truly want for my life, beyond what others expect or want for me?
- What brings me joy, fulfillment, and purpose?
- What goals excite me, even if they don't make sense to others?

By identifying your core values and desires, you create a solid foundation for living authentically. These insights become your guiding principles, helping you make decisions that align with your true self, not what others expect or what society dictates.

How to Prioritize Your Needs Without Guilt

One of the biggest obstacles to living for yourself is the feeling of **guilt** that often arises when we prioritize our own needs over the needs of others. From a young age, we're conditioned to believe that being selfless is virtuous and that putting others first is a moral obligation. While there is certainly a place for kindness and compassion, constantly putting others' needs before your own can lead to burnout, resentment, and a loss of personal fulfillment.

To truly embrace the freedom of living for yourself, you must learn how to **prioritize your needs without guilt**. Here's how:

1. **Recognize That Self-Care Is Not Selfish** Self-care is essential for maintaining your physical, mental, and emotional health. It's not selfish or indulgent—it's a necessity. When you take care of yourself, you are better able to show up for others in a healthy, present, and authentic way. You can't pour from an empty cup, and taking time to recharge isn't something to feel guilty about. In fact, it's a way to ensure that you can give your best to the people and projects that matter to you.

2. **Set Boundaries That Honor Your Needs** Setting healthy boundaries is a crucial part of prioritizing your needs. This might mean saying no to requests that drain your energy, asking for time and space when you need it, or communicating

openly with others about what you're capable of giving at any given time. Boundaries are not walls—they are protective measures that allow you to live authentically without feeling overwhelmed or depleted.

Practice setting boundaries by being clear about your limits. For example, if you're feeling overextended, it's okay to say, "I'd love to help, but I don't have the capacity right now. Let's find another time." Boundaries help you protect your time, energy, and mental well-being.

3. **Understand That People's Reactions Are Not Your Responsibility**
   One of the biggest sources of guilt comes from worrying about how others will react when we prioritize ourselves. We fear that saying no or taking time for ourselves will upset others or lead to conflict. But the truth is, **other people's reactions are not your responsibility**. Everyone is entitled to their own feelings, and while it's important to be compassionate, you cannot control how others respond to your decisions. By prioritizing yourself, you're teaching others how to respect your boundaries and your needs.

4. **Practice Self-Compassion**
   Learning to prioritize yourself without guilt requires practice, and part of that practice is being kind to yourself. It's easy to fall into the trap of self-

criticism, especially when you've spent years prioritizing others. But self-compassion is key to overcoming guilt. Treat yourself with the same kindness and understanding that you would offer a close friend. If you feel guilty, acknowledge that feeling without judgment and gently remind yourself that you are worthy of taking care of your own needs.

5. **Embrace the Power of No** Saying no is one of the most powerful tools you have to protect your time and energy. It's not about rejecting others; it's about **honoring your own needs**. When you say no, you are saying yes to your own well-being and priorities. Learning to say no with confidence—and without guilt—gives you the freedom to live your life according to your own terms.

By following these steps, you can build a life that reflects your true desires and values, without the constant pressure of living for others. The freedom to be you comes when you make the conscious choice to put yourself first, honor your needs, and stop feeling guilty for doing so.

Letting Go at Work

Releasing the Pressure to Meet External Expectations

In the modern workplace, there's often an unspoken pressure to constantly exceed expectations. We are encouraged to be high achievers, always striving for promotions, praise, and perfection. While ambition and hard work are valuable, the relentless pressure to meet external expectations can lead to burnout, dissatisfaction, and a loss of personal fulfillment. This chapter explores how to release that pressure, focus on your own growth, and regain your sense of purpose at work.

At the heart of external expectations is the need for **external validation**—the desire for recognition, praise, and approval from colleagues, managers, and the larger organization. While it's natural to want to be recognized for your contributions, tying your self-worth to the approval of others can create a cycle of stress and anxiety. You may feel as if you're never doing enough, no matter how much you accomplish.

Releasing the pressure to meet external expectations involves rethinking how you define success at work. Instead of measuring your worth based on promotions, salary increases, or the approval of others, shift your focus to internal markers of success—such as your personal growth, your ability to contribute meaningfully, and your satisfaction with your work-life balance.

Start by:

- **Shifting Your Perspective**: Rather than seeing your career as a race for recognition, view it as a journey of personal and professional growth.
- **Redefining Success**: Ask yourself what success looks like for *you*. Is it about having a fulfilling role, gaining new skills, or maintaining a healthy work-life balance? Your definition of success doesn't have to match the one set by others.
- **Releasing Perfectionism**: Understand that perfection is an unrealistic and often paralyzing standard. Focus on doing your best, not being perfect.

When you release the pressure of meeting others' expectations, you open up space to explore your true potential and find more joy and satisfaction in your work.

Creating a Career on Your Own Terms

For many people, career success is defined by external factors: climbing the corporate ladder, receiving promotions, or attaining prestigious titles. But in reality, success in your career is deeply personal. It's about aligning your professional life with your values, passions, and goals. Creating a career on your own terms means letting go of the need to conform to others' definitions of success and designing a career path that fulfills *you*.

Here are some ways to start creating a career on your own terms:

1. **Clarify Your Values and Priorities** Before you can design a career that suits you, you need to understand what truly matters. Do you value flexibility over security? Are you driven by creativity or by making a tangible impact? Understanding your core values will help you make career decisions that align with your true self, rather than simply following the crowd or striving for approval.

2. **Set Intentional Career Goals** Career goals shouldn't just be about promotions or salary increases. Consider what type of work you want to do, the kind of impact you want to have, and the lifestyle you want to maintain. Setting intentional goals allows you to chart a career path that excites and motivates you, rather than one that's dictated by external pressures.

3. **Align Your Work with Your Passions** A fulfilling career is often the result of pursuing work that aligns with your passions and interests. While it's not always possible to immediately

transition into your dream job, there are often ways to incorporate elements of your passions into your current role. Start by identifying the aspects of your work that energize you and look for opportunities to take on more of that work.

4. **Embrace Flexibility and Experimentation** The traditional career path is no longer the only option. Many people are finding success by creating their own businesses, transitioning to freelance work, or taking on unconventional career paths. If the corporate world doesn't align with your vision, consider how you could build a career that gives you more autonomy and flexibility.

By creating a career on your own terms, you free yourself from the constraints of traditional expectations and can pursue work that aligns with who you are, not just who others want you to be.

Setting Boundaries and Saying No with Confidence

One of the most powerful tools in *The Let Them Theory* is learning how to set **boundaries**. Boundaries are essential for maintaining your well-being and creating a career that serves your needs and desires. Yet, many people struggle with saying no, particularly in the workplace. There's often a fear that saying no will be perceived as lazy, uncooperative, or unambitious.

But the truth is, learning to set boundaries and say no with confidence is one of the most effective ways to preserve your time, energy, and focus. Boundaries allow you to prioritize your well-being and ensure that your work aligns with your personal values and goals.

Here's how to set boundaries at work and say no without feeling guilty:

1. **Recognize Your Limits**
   The first step in setting boundaries is recognizing your limits—emotionally, physically, and mentally. When you understand what you can handle and what pushes you beyond your capacity, it becomes easier to say no without guilt. Understand that saying no is a form of self-respect, not selfishness.

2. **Be Direct and Clear**
   When you need to say no, be direct but respectful. You don't need to apologize excessively or offer a lengthy explanation. Simply state your limits and offer an alternative solution if possible. For example: "I'm unable to take on this project right now, but I can help you find someone else who might be available."

3. **Practice Self-Compassion**
   Saying no can be uncomfortable, especially if you're used to people-pleasing or seeking approval. But remember, boundaries are about protecting your time and energy. You don't need to justify or over-

explain your reasons for setting limits. Be kind to yourself and recognize that protecting your own needs is important for your long-term well-being and success.

4. **Build Your Confidence** Confidence in setting boundaries comes with practice. Start small by saying no to low-stakes requests, and gradually build up to more challenging situations. Over time, you'll feel more comfortable asserting your needs and prioritizing your own well-being.

By learning to set boundaries and say no, you take back control of your time, energy, and career. You free yourself from the stress of overcommitment and create space for the work that truly matters to you.

Breaking Free from Fear and Self-Doubt

Why Fear Holds Us Back and How to Overcome It

Fear is one of the most powerful forces in our lives. It can shape our decisions, limit our potential, and keep us stuck in a cycle of inaction. Fear of failure, fear of judgment, fear of the unknown—these are all common barriers that hold us back from pursuing our dreams, taking risks, and embracing opportunities. But while fear is a natural and protective response, it often holds us captive, preventing us from living authentically and fully.

The root of fear is often tied to **the need for control** and **external validation**. We fear what we can't control: how others will perceive us, whether we'll succeed, and how we'll handle rejection or failure. This fear keeps us in our comfort zones, avoiding challenges or changes that could lead to growth.

However, **fear doesn't have to control you**. The Let Them Theory offers a powerful antidote by helping us realize that we don't need to control every outcome or seek approval from others to move forward. The moment we stop allowing fear to dictate our decisions, we regain our power to act freely and confidently.

Here are a few strategies for overcoming fear:

1. **Acknowledge the Fear, Don't Ignore It** Fear isn't something that should be repressed or ignored—it's a signal that something matters to us. Acknowledge the fear and understand its source. Is it fear of failure? Fear of rejection? Recognizing what you're afraid of helps you address it head-on, rather than avoiding it.

2. **Challenge Your Limiting Beliefs** Often, the fears we experience are based on false or exaggerated beliefs. We might fear that we're not good enough, that others will judge us, or that we'll fail catastrophically. Start by questioning these beliefs. Ask yourself: "What evidence do I have that this will happen?" Most of the time, the worst-case scenarios we fear are highly unlikely.

3. **Take Small, Courageous Steps** Overcoming fear doesn't mean eliminating it entirely—it means taking action despite it. Start with small steps that push you slightly out of your comfort zone. Each small victory will build your confidence and show you that fear doesn't have to be an obstacle to progress.

4. **Focus on What You Can Control** The Let Them Theory emphasizes the importance of letting go of things beyond your control. Focus your energy on what you *can* control—your actions,

your mindset, and your reactions. When you stop worrying about things that are out of your hands, fear loses its grip on you.

By reframing your relationship with fear and taking proactive steps to face it, you can break free from its hold and move toward your goals with greater confidence and clarity.

Transforming Self-Doubt into Confidence

Self-doubt is another pervasive force that holds us back from achieving our potential. It whispers to us that we're not good enough, that we don't deserve success, or that we're bound to fail. Like fear, self-doubt is a natural response, but when it's left unchecked, it can paralyze us from taking action.

The Let Them Theory offers a way to **transform self-doubt** into confidence by shifting our focus from external validation to internal validation. Instead of waiting for others to approve of us or constantly seeking reassurance, we can learn to trust ourselves and our abilities.

Here's how to transform self-doubt into confidence:

1. **Recognize That Self-Doubt Is Normal** Everyone experiences self-doubt from time to time—it's part of being human. The key is not to see self-doubt as a sign of weakness or failure but as a

natural response to stepping outside of your comfort zone. Rather than running from self-doubt, acknowledge it as a sign that you are pushing yourself to grow.

2. **Shift Your Focus from Perfection to Progress** Often, self-doubt arises when we feel that we aren't doing something perfectly or meeting our own high standards. Shift your focus from perfection to progress. Celebrate small wins and incremental growth rather than expecting immediate, flawless results.

3. **Develop a Growth Mindset** Cultivate a mindset that sees challenges and setbacks as opportunities for growth, rather than as failures. When you view obstacles as part of the learning process, you begin to trust in your ability to overcome them. **Self-doubt** loses its power when you see each experience as a stepping stone toward your personal development.

4. **Build a Positive Internal Dialogue** The way you speak to yourself matters. Start to replace negative self-talk with affirmations and statements that support your growth. For example, replace "I'm not good enough" with "I am capable, and I'm learning every day." Positive self-talk fosters a stronger sense of self-belief and empowers you to take action, even when doubt arises.

By transforming self-doubt into confidence, you shift from a place of fear and uncertainty to a place of self-assurance. You become empowered to take risks, try new things, and step into opportunities with trust in your abilities.

Using the Let Them Theory to Build Resilience

Resilience is the ability to bounce back from setbacks, adapt to change, and keep moving forward despite challenges. It's an essential skill for navigating life's ups and downs, and it's something that anyone can build over time. The Let Them Theory offers a powerful framework for building resilience by encouraging you to **release control over things that are out of your hands** and focus on what you can control: your mindset, your actions, and your responses.

Here's how to use the Let Them Theory to build resilience:

1. **Let Go of What You Can't Control**
   The first step in building resilience is recognizing that not everything is within your control. When faced with setbacks or challenges, focus on what you can change and let go of what you can't. For example, you can't control the behavior of others, but you can control how you respond. This shift in mindset frees you from feeling powerless and helps you move forward with confidence.

2. **Embrace Challenges as Opportunities** Resilience is built through adversity. Instead of avoiding challenges or seeing them as roadblocks, view them as opportunities for growth. Ask yourself: "What can I learn from this situation?" Every difficulty you face is an opportunity to grow stronger and more adaptable.

3. **Practice Self-Compassion** Resilient people don't beat themselves up when things go wrong. They practice self-compassion, understanding that mistakes and setbacks are part of the process. Be kind to yourself when things don't go as planned, and use those moments as stepping stones to become stronger.

4. **Cultivate a Support System** Building resilience doesn't mean going it alone. Surround yourself with people who support and uplift you, whether it's family, friends, mentors, or colleagues. A strong support system provides the emotional resources you need to recover from setbacks and keep moving forward.

5. **Focus on the Present Moment** Resilience requires the ability to stay grounded in the present, rather than getting overwhelmed by past mistakes or future worries. Use mindfulness practices to center yourself in the here and now, focusing on the next step you can take rather than

getting lost in what could have been or what might be.

By embracing the Let Them Theory and focusing on what you can control, you can build the resilience necessary to face life's challenges with confidence and strength. You'll develop the ability to bounce back from setbacks, adapt to change, and keep pursuing your goals, no matter what obstacles arise.

Letting Go of People's Expectations in Relationships

How to Stop Pleasing Everyone

One of the most powerful barriers to authentic relationships is the desire to please others. From childhood, we are often conditioned to seek approval from our family, friends, partners, and society. Whether it's through seeking validation, avoiding conflict, or conforming to expectations, we end up sacrificing our own needs and desires in order to keep others happy.

This constant people-pleasing behavior can create deep emotional exhaustion and lead to resentment. It often stems from a fear of rejection, the desire for acceptance, or the need to feel valued by others. The problem is that no matter how much you try to please others, it's impossible to meet everyone's expectations. People's desires, opinions, and needs constantly shift, making it an impossible goal to satisfy everyone all the time.

The **Let Them Theory** offers a profound shift: **Let them** have their own opinions, preferences, and expectations, but don't let these dictate your behavior or your happiness. It's not selfish to put your needs first—it's necessary for maintaining healthy, authentic relationships.

Here's how to stop pleasing everyone:

1. **Identify the Root of People-Pleasing** Start by understanding why you feel compelled to please others. Is it out of fear of rejection, guilt, or a desire to be liked? Recognizing the emotional triggers behind people-pleasing behavior is the first step toward releasing its grip on you.

2. **Shift Your Focus to Your Own Needs** People-pleasing often comes from putting other people's needs ahead of your own. Start asking yourself, "What do I need right now?" or "What feels right for me?" Focus on meeting your own needs before attempting to fulfill the needs of others.

3. **Practice Saying No** Saying "no" is one of the most powerful tools in breaking free from the need to please everyone. It's essential to learn that saying no to others doesn't mean saying no to the relationship—it means saying yes to your own boundaries, time, and energy.

4. **Embrace Discomfort** Saying no or not meeting someone's expectations may feel uncomfortable at first, but it's a necessary part of asserting your own autonomy. Over time, you'll become more comfortable with discomfort, knowing that your emotional well-being is worth prioritizing.

By letting go of the need to please everyone, you free yourself to build relationships based on mutual respect, authenticity, and shared values, rather than the constant dance of meeting others' ever-changing expectations.

Building Authentic and Fulfilling Relationships

Authenticity is the foundation of any meaningful, fulfilling relationship. Yet, many of us enter relationships with a facade, trying to be what others want us to be rather than showing up as our true selves. This often leads to superficial connections, misunderstandings, and a lack of genuine intimacy. The Let Them Theory encourages you to build relationships where **you can be yourself, and others can be themselves**, without needing to conform to external standards or expectations.

Building authentic relationships requires courage, self-awareness, and vulnerability. It's about showing up fully, being honest about your needs and desires, and creating connections based on mutual understanding and respect. When you stop trying to mold yourself into someone you're not to fit in, you open the door to deeper, more fulfilling connections.

Here are some strategies for building authentic relationships:

1. **Be Honest About Who You Are** Authenticity starts with being honest with yourself and others. Instead of trying to conform to someone else's idea of who you should be, embrace your uniqueness. Share your true thoughts, feelings, and experiences without fear of judgment. Authenticity fosters trust and encourages others to be authentic as well.

2. **Cultivate Vulnerability** Vulnerability is often seen as a weakness, but in reality, it's the key to deep, meaningful connections. When you allow yourself to be vulnerable—by sharing your fears, struggles, and aspirations—you invite others to do the same. This mutual openness creates strong bonds and builds intimacy in relationships.

3. **Invest in Relationships That Align with Your Values**
Not all relationships are meant to last, and that's okay. Focus on building connections with people who share your values and who support you for who you truly are, not for who they want you to be. Authentic relationships are built on mutual respect, trust, and shared growth.

4. **Let Go of Toxic Relationships** Authentic relationships thrive when both parties are committed to growth and mutual respect. If

someone in your life consistently demands that you sacrifice your own needs, or makes you feel unworthy of being yourself, it's time to let go. The **Let Them Theory** encourages you to release toxic relationships that drain your energy and focus on those that nourish your soul.

The Role of Communication and Boundaries in Healthy Relationships

Effective communication and clear boundaries are the cornerstones of healthy, fulfilling relationships. Without them, misunderstandings, resentment, and frustration are inevitable. In the context of the **Let Them Theory**, communication and boundaries empower you to assert your needs, respect the needs of others, and maintain a sense of autonomy in your relationships.

1. **Clear and Honest Communication**
   Communication is more than just talking—it's about being able to express your feelings, desires, and boundaries in a way that is both honest and respectful. When you communicate clearly, you ensure that both parties understand each other's expectations and needs.

   - **Be Direct, But Compassionate**: When you need to express something important, do so with clarity and respect. It's possible to be honest without being hurtful.

- **Listen Actively**: Good communication also involves listening. Practice active listening by giving your full attention to the speaker, acknowledging their feelings, and responding thoughtfully.

2. **Establishing Boundaries**
   Boundaries are essential for maintaining healthy relationships. They help you protect your time, energy, and emotional well-being while also showing respect for others. Setting boundaries is a way of letting people know what is and isn't acceptable to you, without the guilt or fear of judgment.

   - **Identify Your Limits**: Start by recognizing your emotional, physical, and mental limits. What are the things that drain you, or make you uncomfortable? Once you identify them, you can communicate your boundaries clearly.

   - **Say No Without Guilt**: Boundaries require the courage to say no when something doesn't align with your needs or values. Saying no isn't a rejection of the other person—it's an act of self-respect.

   - **Respect Others' Boundaries**: Healthy relationships are built on mutual respect. Just as you have boundaries, so do others.

Honor their boundaries as you would expect them to honor yours.

3. **Navigating Conflict with Respect**
   Conflict is inevitable in any relationship, but how you handle it can make or break the relationship. When conflict arises, focus on addressing the issue rather than attacking the person. Approach disagreements with curiosity and a willingness to understand, rather than a need to be right.

   - **Stay Calm and Open**: When emotions run high, it's easy to get defensive. Take a step back, breathe, and approach the conversation with a mindset of understanding.
   - **Seek Win-Win Solutions**: Look for solutions that honor both your needs and the needs of the other person. The goal is to find a resolution that works for everyone, not just one person's agenda.

By prioritizing clear communication and healthy boundaries, you create relationships that are grounded in mutual respect, understanding, and freedom—allowing both you and the other person to **be yourselves** without the weight of external expectations.

Creating the Love You Deserve

Breaking Free from Toxic Relationship Patterns

Toxic relationship patterns can silently erode our sense of self-worth and prevent us from experiencing the love we deserve. Whether it's staying in unhealthy relationships out of fear, guilt, or a desire to "fix" someone, many of us find ourselves stuck in cycles that drain our energy and undermine our happiness. These patterns often stem from unresolved past experiences, unmet emotional needs, or a deep-rooted belief that we're unworthy of better treatment.

One of the most liberating aspects of the **Let Them Theory** is recognizing that **we cannot change others**, but we do have the power to change how we engage in relationships. Letting go of toxic patterns requires us to take a hard look at our behaviors, boundaries, and expectations, and consciously choose to create healthier dynamics in our relationships.

Here's how to break free from toxic relationship patterns:

1. **Acknowledge the Patterns**
   The first step in breaking free from toxic relationships is recognizing the patterns you've been repeating. Are you constantly attracting

partners who are emotionally unavailable? Do you ignore red flags in favor of avoiding loneliness? Take an honest look at your past relationships and identify any recurring themes. Acknowledging these patterns is the first step toward breaking the cycle.

2. **Set Clear Boundaries**
   Toxic relationships often thrive when boundaries are blurred or non-existent. To stop these patterns, you must establish and enforce clear boundaries. This might mean saying "no" to behaviors you've tolerated in the past or cutting ties with people who continually disrespect your limits.

3. **Heal from Past Trauma**
   Often, toxic patterns are rooted in unresolved emotional wounds. Whether from childhood, previous relationships, or unhealed trauma, these past experiences can shape the way we relate to others. Seeking therapy, engaging in self-reflection, and working on healing from these wounds can help you break the hold of past patterns and step into healthier relational dynamics.

4. **Choose to Let Go of Toxic Relationships**
   The hardest part of breaking free from toxic patterns is the decision to let go of people who no longer serve your well-being. Letting go is an act of self-love—it's about honoring your worth and recognizing that you deserve better. The **Let Them**

Theory empowers you to release toxic relationships and make space for healthier, more loving connections.

By consciously choosing to break free from toxic patterns, you free yourself to create the love you deserve—a love that nurtures, supports, and inspires you.

How to Cultivate Healthy, Loving Relationships with Yourself and Others

At the core of creating the love you deserve is cultivating a **healthy relationship with yourself**. We can't expect others to treat us with respect, kindness, and love if we don't first offer those things to ourselves. The foundation of all healthy relationships—romantic, familial, or platonic—rests on self-love, self-acceptance, and self-compassion.

Here's how to cultivate loving relationships with yourself and others:

1. **Practice Self-Love and Acceptance** Self-love is not about narcissism or vanity—it's about treating yourself with the same care, respect, and kindness you would show a loved one. This involves being kind to yourself when you make mistakes, accepting your flaws, and recognizing your inherent worth. **Self-acceptance** means embracing all parts of yourself, including your

imperfections, and acknowledging that you are enough just as you are.

2. **Develop Emotional Awareness and Intelligence** Emotional intelligence is crucial for healthy relationships. It involves recognizing, understanding, and managing your own emotions, as well as empathizing with the emotions of others. When you can navigate your own feelings and respond with empathy, you create a space for deeper connection and understanding in your relationships.

3. **Communicate Openly and Honestly** Healthy relationships are built on open, honest communication. This means expressing your thoughts, feelings, and needs clearly, without fear of judgment or rejection. It also means being a good listener—creating a safe space for others to share their thoughts and feelings without fear of dismissal. Good communication fosters trust and intimacy, essential components of any loving relationship.

4. **Nurture Your Relationships** Relationships require effort, time, and nurturing. This means showing appreciation for your partner, friends, or family, offering support when needed, and investing in quality time together. Don't take

your relationships for granted; actively work to cultivate love, respect, and mutual care.

5. **Surround Yourself with Positive, Supportive People**
   The people we surround ourselves with deeply influence our emotional well-being. If you want to create the love you deserve, it's essential to build a support network of people who lift you up, respect your boundaries, and encourage your growth. Seek out relationships that are based on mutual respect, trust, and shared values.

By cultivating a loving relationship with yourself and fostering healthy connections with others, you create a life filled with love, respect, and fulfillment. This is the foundation of the love you truly deserve.

Letting Go of Unrealistic Expectations in Love

Unrealistic expectations can be one of the most damaging forces in romantic relationships. We may enter relationships with a **fantasy** of what our partner "should" be like, based on societal ideals, past experiences, or romanticized images of love. These expectations often set us up for disappointment, frustration, and feelings of inadequacy.

The **Let Them Theory** encourages us to let go of these unrealistic ideals and embrace the reality of love as a dynamic, evolving connection. True love isn't about perfection—it's about acceptance, understanding, and growth together.

Here's how to let go of unrealistic expectations in love:

1. **Accept Imperfection**
   No one is perfect. Relationships are messy, complicated, and require compromise. Accepting that both you and your partner have flaws will help you approach love with a sense of grace and understanding, rather than constantly seeking perfection.

2. **Release the Fantasy of "The One"**
   Many of us grow up with the idea that there is one perfect person out there meant for us. While a deep connection with a partner is important, releasing the myth of "the one" helps you embrace the beauty of growing together, rather than seeking someone who fulfills all your fantasies.

3. **Communicate Your Needs Realistically**
   Instead of expecting your partner to read your mind or meet every emotional need, focus on clear, honest communication. Express your needs without expecting them to be met in an idealized way—recognize that relationships require flexibility, effort, and compromise.

4. **Embrace Growth Together** Relationships are not static—they evolve as both partners grow individually and together. Let go of the need to control or fix your partner, and instead, focus on growing together. Support each other's goals, dreams, and personal development, and celebrate the journey of building a life together.

By letting go of unrealistic expectations, you create the space for love to unfold naturally—rooted in acceptance, growth, and mutual respect.

Creating the love you deserve begins with letting go—of toxic patterns, unrealistic expectations, and the need for perfection. Through self-awareness, communication, and healthy boundaries, you can cultivate authentic, loving relationships with yourself and others. The **Let Them Theory** empowers you to embrace love on your own terms, free from the limitations of external pressures or past wounds. As you release control and let go of what no longer serves you, you make room for the love that is truly meant for you—abundant, fulfilling, and real.

Building a Life of Joy and Fulfillment

The Secret to Fulfilling Your Own Dreams, Not Others'

In a world where external expectations are constantly imposed on us, it's easy to get caught up in the pursuit of other people's dreams. From parents and teachers to societal pressures and cultural norms, we are often taught to chase after goals that may not truly resonate with our authentic selves. The secret to living a life of joy and fulfillment lies in the ability to **focus on fulfilling your own dreams, not someone else's**.

The **Let Them Theory** emphasizes the importance of reclaiming your personal power and letting go of the need to live up to the expectations of others. This is not to say that you should disregard the opinions of those you love or the advice of mentors—but you must learn to discern whose dreams you are truly chasing.

Here are steps to start fulfilling your own dreams:

1. **Identify What Truly Matters to You** Begin by reflecting on your values, passions, and desires. What do you truly care about? What excites you, even if others might not understand it? To find your own path, you need to first identify what

makes you come alive, independent of anyone else's expectations or opinions.

2. **Let Go of Comparison**
   In today's world of social media and constant connection, it's easy to compare ourselves to others and feel like we're falling behind. But **comparison steals joy**. The journey to fulfillment isn't about competing with others; it's about following your own unique path. Stop looking to others for validation, and instead focus on what feels right for you.

3. **Clarify Your Goals**
   It's important to set clear, personal goals that reflect your dreams, not someone else's vision for you. Whether it's in your career, relationships, personal growth, or hobbies, define what success looks like for you. The clearer your vision, the easier it will be to align your actions with your values.

4. **Release the Need for Approval**
   One of the biggest obstacles to pursuing your own dreams is the fear of disapproval. This fear often prevents us from making bold choices or taking risks. When you choose to fulfill your own dreams, you may face criticism or disappointment from others. But **releasing the need for approval** from anyone but yourself is key to living an authentic, fulfilling life.

When you stop measuring your success by the standards of others and focus on your own passions and desires, you open the door to a life that feels more meaningful and joyful.

Focusing on What Truly Matters to You

In the pursuit of a fulfilling life, it's easy to get distracted by the hustle and bustle of daily life—obligations, deadlines, and the pressure to keep up with everyone around you. **Distractions** can pull us away from what really matters. Whether it's trying to meet the expectations of others or getting caught up in a cycle of busyness, the key to fulfillment is **focusing on what truly matters to you**.

The Let Them Theory encourages you to prioritize your happiness, peace, and personal growth above all else. This is not about being selfish—it's about making conscious choices that reflect your deepest values and desires.

Here's how to focus on what truly matters:

1. **Identify Your Core Values** Take time to reflect on what matters most to you in life. What are your **non-negotiables**? Whether it's integrity, family, creativity, health, or adventure, identifying your core values gives you a compass for making decisions and setting priorities. When

you know what truly matters, it's easier to say "no" to things that don't align with your values.

2. **Eliminate Time Wasters**
   In order to focus on what matters, you must eliminate the distractions and time-wasters that steal your energy. Whether it's endless scrolling on social media, overcommitting to obligations, or staying in relationships that drain you, **clearing out the clutter** from your life creates space for the things that matter most.

3. **Set Boundaries**
   Setting boundaries is crucial to protecting your time and energy. Let go of the need to please everyone or overextend yourself. By setting clear boundaries, you prioritize your needs and protect the space you need to focus on your own happiness and personal growth.

4. **Practice Mindfulness and Presence**
   Focusing on what matters also involves being present in the moment. Practice mindfulness by engaging fully in the activities that bring you joy, whether it's spending quality time with loved ones, pursuing a passion, or simply enjoying nature. The more present you are, the more you'll appreciate the richness of life.

How to Align Your Daily Habits with Your Happiness Goals

To build a life of joy and fulfillment, you must **align your daily habits with your happiness goals**. It's not enough to have a vision for the life you want—you must also take consistent action that supports your goals. Daily habits shape the course of your life, and small, intentional changes can make a huge difference over time.

The **Let Them Theory** emphasizes the importance of taking responsibility for your own life and happiness. When you align your daily actions with your values and desires, you create a life that feels fulfilling, purposeful, and joyful.

Here are strategies for aligning your daily habits with your happiness goals:

1. **Start Your Day with Intention**
   The way you begin your day sets the tone for everything that follows. Start your morning by setting an intention for how you want to feel and what you want to accomplish. Whether it's practicing gratitude, setting a clear goal, or simply visualizing your ideal day, **intentionality** helps you stay focused on your happiness throughout the day.

2. **Create Routines That Support Your Well-being**
   Establish daily habits that nurture your body, mind, and spirit. This might include exercise, meditation,

journaling, reading, or spending time in nature. When you make self-care a daily priority, you increase your overall sense of well-being and happiness.

3. **Break Down Big Goals into Small Actions** The key to achieving your dreams is taking consistent action. Break your larger goals into manageable, daily tasks. By doing something each day that moves you closer to your happiness goals, you create momentum and progress over time.

4. **Celebrate Small Wins** Progress doesn't always come in big leaps—it's often the small wins that make the biggest impact. Celebrate your successes along the way, no matter how small they seem. Acknowledging these wins reinforces your commitment to building a fulfilling life.

5. **Reflect and Adjust** Life is ever-changing, and so are your goals. Make time for regular reflection on your journey—what's working, what's not, and where you can make adjustments. Being flexible and open to change allows you to stay aligned with what truly brings you joy and fulfillment.

Letting Go of Stress and Distractions

Identifying Your Energy Drains and Eliminating Them

In the modern world, it's easy to feel overwhelmed. Between work, social obligations, personal goals, and the constant stream of information we're exposed to, it can seem like there's no time or energy left for what truly matters. But the truth is, much of the stress and distraction we experience is self-imposed. We often overlook the **energy drains** in our lives—things that sap our focus, enthusiasm, and motivation—because we've become accustomed to them.

The first step in letting go of stress and distractions is **identifying what drains your energy**. These drains can come in many forms, from toxic relationships and negative thought patterns to poorly managed time and constant multitasking.

Here's how to identify and eliminate your energy drains:

1. **Assess Your Relationships**
   Take stock of the people in your life. Are there relationships that leave you feeling drained or emotionally depleted? Toxic relationships—whether personal or professional—can be a major

energy drain. Let go of relationships that no longer serve you, or establish boundaries to protect your energy.

2. **Examine Your Habits**
   Reflect on your daily routines. Are there habits that consume your time without adding value to your life? For instance, mindlessly scrolling through social media, overcommitting to tasks, or getting caught up in unnecessary drama can all be draining. Make a conscious effort to eliminate time-wasting activities that don't align with your goals.

3. **Minimize External Distractions**
   Our environment plays a big role in how much stress we feel. Consider your work environment, home space, and digital landscape. Are they cluttered, disorganized, or filled with distractions? A clean, organized space can help you feel more grounded and focused. Additionally, **digital detoxes**—periods of time when you disconnect from email, social media, and other online platforms—can also help restore your mental clarity.

4. **Prioritize Self-Care**
   Self-care is not just about physical rest—it's about emotional and mental nourishment. Regularly taking time for yourself, whether through hobbies, rest, or spending time in nature, can help you

recharge and regain the energy you need to focus on what matters.

By identifying and eliminating these energy drains, you can reclaim your time and emotional resources, which will help you reducc stress and increase focus.

Building Resilience Against Everyday Stressors

Stress is inevitable. We can't control all the factors that contribute to stress, but we **can control how we respond**. The key to dealing with stress effectively is building **resilience**—the ability to bounce back from setbacks, remain calm under pressure, and maintain a positive outlook even in the face of adversity.

Resilience isn't something we're born with; it's a skill we can develop over time. It requires a mindset shift and consistent practice. By learning how to manage stress effectively, you can protect your mental health and continue pursuing your goals with confidence, even when life throws curveballs.

Here are strategies for building resilience:

1. **Practice Emotional Awareness** Resilience starts with understanding your emotions. When stress arises, pause to identify what you're feeling—whether it's frustration, anxiety, or overwhelm. This awareness allows you to detach

from the emotions and take a more measured, rational approach to the situation.

2. **Reframe Your Perspective** The way we perceive stress can either help or hinder our resilience. Instead of viewing stress as something that harms you, try reframing it as a challenge or an opportunity for growth. Research has shown that when we see stress as something we can handle, we are more likely to perform better under pressure and recover more quickly.

3. **Develop Healthy Coping Mechanisms** Resilience isn't just about enduring stress; it's about coping with it in healthy ways. Establish coping strategies like deep breathing, mindfulness, exercise, or journaling to help you manage stress in the moment. Regularly engaging in activities that promote relaxation can also help you build a stronger foundation for resilience.

4. **Build a Support Network** No one should have to go through stress alone. Cultivate a network of friends, family, or colleagues you can turn to for support during tough times. Having people who listen, understand, and offer guidance can make a significant difference in your ability to cope with stress.

5. **Practice Gratitude** Resilience thrives in an attitude of gratitude. Even

during stressful times, focusing on what's going well in your life can help shift your mindset. Gratitude reminds us that, despite challenges, we have things to be thankful for—and this perspective can help us bounce back more quickly.

Building resilience isn't about avoiding stress altogether; it's about learning how to navigate it with strength and grace, knowing that challenges are part of the journey.

Staying Focused on Your True Path Amidst Chaos

Life can feel chaotic at times—work pressures, family obligations, and unexpected events can all pull us in different directions. In the midst of this chaos, it's easy to lose sight of what truly matters to us and get caught up in the whirlwind of demands. However, the **Let Them Theory** teaches us that by letting go of the things we cannot control, we can focus more on the path we've chosen for ourselves.

Staying focused on your true path amidst chaos requires intentionality, clarity, and discipline. Here's how to stay on track:

1. **Clarify Your Long-Term Vision**
   In the midst of everyday chaos, it's easy to get caught up in immediate concerns and short-term distractions. Take a step back and remind yourself

of your long-term goals. What is your ultimate vision for your life? Keeping this vision in mind helps you make decisions that align with your true desires, rather than reacting to external pressures.

2. **Break Down Big Goals Into Smaller Steps** When chaos is swirling around you, the big picture can seem overwhelming. Break your long-term goals into manageable, actionable steps. Focusing on one step at a time allows you to make consistent progress without becoming overwhelmed.

3. **Embrace Flexibility** While it's important to stay focused, it's also crucial to embrace flexibility. Life is unpredictable, and you may need to adjust your plans as circumstances change. Resilience comes from your ability to stay adaptable while still keeping your eyes on your ultimate goals.

4. **Create Space for Reflection** In times of stress or chaos, it's essential to regularly reflect on your progress, your emotions, and your priorities. Set aside time each day or week to assess where you are on your path. Are you still aligned with your values and goals? Is there anything you need to change or let go of? Reflection helps you stay grounded and focused amidst the noise.

5. **Trust the Process** Trust that even when things don't go as planned,

you're still moving forward in the right direction. Trust that every setback, every challenge, is part of your journey, not an obstacle to your success. Keeping faith in your path allows you to persevere and stay focused on your long-term happiness and fulfillment.

Staying focused on your true path amidst chaos is not about avoiding distractions or controlling every aspect of your life; it's about remaining grounded in your vision and knowing that, with resilience and clarity, you can navigate through any storm.

Defining Your Own Success

Letting Go of the Conventional Definition of Success

For as long as most of us can remember, we've been told what success looks like. Success is often defined by societal standards—wealth, status, career achievement, a perfect family, or a curated social media presence. These external benchmarks of success, while admirable in their own right, may not align with your deepest desires or values. **The Let Them Theory** encourages you to step away from these conventional definitions and **reclaim your personal vision of success**.

The truth is, success is subjective. What might be fulfilling for one person could be unimportant to another. So, the first step in defining your success is to **let go of other people's definitions**. Stop measuring yourself against a standard that may not reflect your true aspirations.

Here's how to let go of the conventional definition of success:

1. **Challenge Societal Norms**
   Take a hard look at the societal definitions of success—high-paying jobs, prestige, or a life that seems perfect on the outside. Ask yourself: Are

these the things I truly value? Are they aligned with my personal vision of a meaningful life? This might require questioning deeply held beliefs, such as the idea that financial success equates to happiness or that career achievement defines your worth.

2. **Shift from External Validation to Internal Fulfillment**
   Most traditional definitions of success focus on external markers like recognition, promotions, or material wealth. While these things are not inherently bad, they can cause a constant cycle of seeking validation from others. The key is to start focusing on **internal fulfillment**—how your work, relationships, and experiences make you feel, rather than how they make you appear to others.

3. **Release the Pressure of Perfection**
   Society often portrays success as a perfect, linear journey: a flawless career, a happy family life, and endless accomplishments. But **perfection is an illusion**, and the pressure to meet that ideal can be crippling. Let go of the idea that success means having everything "together" at all times. Embrace the messy, unpredictable journey of life and recognize that success is about growth, learning, and becoming more of who you truly are.

By **letting go of the conventional definition of success**, you free yourself to create a path that is authentic to your life and goals.

Crafting Your Personal Path to Achievement and Happiness

Your personal path to achievement and happiness doesn't need to follow anyone else's blueprint. In fact, it's far more powerful when it's uniquely tailored to you—your passions, values, and purpose. Once you release external expectations, you can begin to craft your **personal vision of success**.

Here's how to create your own path to achievement and happiness:

1. **Identify Your True Values and Passions** To build a fulfilling life, you must first know what you truly value. What excites you? What are you passionate about? Is it creativity, family, community, adventure, or making a difference in the world? Spend time reflecting on what lights you up and how you want to spend your time. When your actions align with your values and passions, you're much more likely to experience a sense of fulfillment and happiness.

2. **Set Goals That Reflect Your Vision, Not Someone Else's**
   Once you've identified your values, set goals that reflect them. These goals should align with what matters most to you, not what others think you should achieve. Whether it's a career milestone, a personal development goal, or a relationship aspiration, make sure your goals are meaningful to you. This will help you stay motivated and inspired, even when the path becomes challenging.

3. **Be Open to Change and Adaptation**
   The path to success is rarely a straight line. Life will present challenges, opportunities, and detours. **Flexibility** and adaptability are crucial as you work toward your goals. If something no longer aligns with your values or brings you joy, don't be afraid to change direction. The Let Them Theory is about staying true to yourself, even if it means constantly redefining your path as you grow and evolve.

4. **Embrace the Journey, Not Just the Destination**
   Often, we fixate on the end goal—be it a promotion, a dream home, or financial independence—but **the real value lies in the journey**. Celebrate the small wins, the lessons learned, and the growth you experience along the way. The process of pursuing your goals is just as important as the outcomes. Cultivate joy in the present moment, rather than

postponing happiness until you "arrive" at some future destination.

5. **Align Your Life with Your Purpose** Ultimately, true success comes from aligning your daily life with your **purpose**. Your purpose is the underlying reason behind everything you do, whether it's creating meaningful work, fostering relationships, or contributing to something greater than yourself. When you feel connected to your purpose, your life feels more fulfilling, and you're more resilient in the face of challenges.

By crafting your own personal path, you create a life that resonates with your true desires and brings you lasting joy and fulfillment.

How to Celebrate Your Wins Without External Approval

Too often, we look for external validation to confirm our success. Whether it's praise from others, a bonus at work, or a like on social media, we seek approval from the outside world to feel validated. But relying on others' approval for our sense of achievement is fleeting, and it can prevent us from truly enjoying our accomplishments.

The **Let Them Theory** encourages you to **celebrate your wins** on your own terms, without waiting for permission or approval from others.

Here's how to celebrate your wins without relying on external validation:

1. **Acknowledge Your Own Accomplishments**
   Before you seek approval from others, take a moment to recognize and appreciate your achievements. Whether it's finishing a project, reaching a personal milestone, or overcoming a challenge, give yourself credit. **Self-acknowledgment** is key to building self-esteem and reinforcing your sense of worth.

2. **Celebrate in a Way That Feels Right for You**
   Celebrating doesn't have to mean throwing a big party or sharing the news with everyone you know. It can be as simple as taking time to reflect, treating yourself to something meaningful, or enjoying a quiet moment of appreciation. **Celebrate in a way that feels authentic to you**, rather than trying to meet someone else's expectations for celebration.

3. **Share Your Success with Those Who Truly Support You**
   While external validation shouldn't be the driving force behind your celebrations, it can still feel meaningful to share your wins with loved ones who support you. Choose people who genuinely

celebrate your achievements and want to see you succeed. Their support will feel more rewarding because it's based on **mutual respect and understanding**.

4. **Use Your Wins as Fuel for the Next Step** Celebrating doesn't mean resting on your laurels indefinitely—it's about using your successes as **motivation** to continue moving forward. Every achievement, no matter how small, is a step on the path to your bigger vision. After celebrating, reflect on what you've learned and how it can propel you toward your next goal.

By **celebrating your wins without external approval**, you build a deeper connection to your own sense of fulfillment and create a sustainable source of motivation and joy.

The Power of Letting Them in Practice

Real-Life Stories of Transformation

The true power of Letting Them comes to life not just in theory, but in the real, tangible results it produces in people's lives. When individuals begin to apply the principles of the Let Them Theory, they often experience profound transformations—both in their personal lives and in their professional endeavors.

These transformations aren't just about grand success stories or dramatic overhauls. Instead, they reflect the quiet shifts that occur when people stop fighting against the forces outside their control and start focusing on what they can influence. Here are some real-life stories of people who have embraced the Let Them Theory and how it radically changed their approach to life:

Rachel's Journey from Burnout to Balance Rachel, a corporate executive, was caught in a constant cycle of burnout. She spent years climbing the corporate ladder, striving for promotions and accolades, but was increasingly dissatisfied with her work and personal life. She felt like she was constantly seeking approval from her boss, colleagues, and even her family. This led to anxiety, stress, and a deep sense of inadequacy.

After discovering the Let Them Theory, Rachel realized that she had been giving her energy to things outside her control—other people's expectations, company politics, and a never-ending to-do list. By embracing the power of letting go, Rachel was able to create better boundaries, stop people-pleasing, and prioritize her own needs. She reduced her hours, focused on work that she genuinely enjoyed, and started making time for self-care. Slowly but surely, she reclaimed her joy, stopped living for external validation, and found balance between her career and personal life.

Ben's Shift from Fear to Confidence Ben was a freelance writer who constantly battled self-doubt. He was always comparing his work to that of other writers and feared rejection with every pitch he submitted. He was paralyzed by the thought of not measuring up and often second-guessed himself, leaving him stuck in a cycle of procrastination.

By embracing the Let Them Theory, Ben learned to let go of the fear of judgment and stop comparing himself to others. He began focusing solely on the value he could offer through his writing and started trusting his voice. The result? He landed his dream clients, gained confidence in his work, and found joy in the creative process without the constant worry about other people's opinions. His productivity skyrocketed, and so did his income.

Maria's Transformation in Relationships Maria had always struggled in her relationships, feeling like she had to meet everyone's expectations in order to feel loved and accepted. She would overextend herself for friends and family, constantly worried about how others viewed her. This led to resentment, burnout, and strained relationships.

After learning the Let Them Theory, Maria began to release the need to please everyone. She set healthy boundaries, stopped feeling responsible for others' emotions, and focused on cultivating relationships that were authentic and fulfilling. As a result, her friendships deepened, her romantic relationships flourished, and she felt more at peace with herself. By allowing herself to prioritize her own needs without guilt, Maria found that her relationships became more supportive and balanced.

These stories show how the Let Them Theory isn't just a theoretical concept—it's a life-changing practice that empowers people to break free from external pressures, reclaim their autonomy, and create the life they truly want.

How the Let Them Theory Has Changed People's Lives

The Let Them Theory has already helped millions of people worldwide overcome the limitations imposed by societal expectations, fear, and external pressures. Here's how it has changed people's lives:

More Control Over Their Own Happiness By letting go of other people's judgments and expectations, individuals have taken back control over their own happiness. They've stopped living for others and started prioritizing their own desires, values, and well-being.

Increased Confidence and Self-Worth People who have embraced the Let Them Theory report a significant boost in their self-esteem. By releasing the need for external validation and self-criticism, they've learned to validate themselves and pursue their goals with confidence.

Stronger Relationships Letting go of the pressure to please everyone has led to healthier, more authentic relationships. People have learned how to set boundaries, communicate effectively, and build connections that are based on mutual respect rather than obligation.

Reduced Stress and Anxiety Releasing the need for control and letting go of the overwhelming weight of other people's opinions has led to lower levels of stress and anxiety. People are now able to focus on what truly matters to them, leading to a greater sense of peace and well-being.

Greater Success and Fulfillment Ironically, many individuals have found that when they stop chasing after conventional definitions of success and start creating their own paths, they actually achieve greater success in ways that are meaningful to them. Their careers, passions, and personal lives flourish because they are aligned with their authentic selves.

How to Apply Let Them Every Day to Stay on Track

Implementing the Let Them Theory isn't a one-time event—it's a practice that requires daily commitment. In order to stay on track and continue reaping the benefits of this powerful mindset, here are some actionable steps you can incorporate into your daily routine:

Practice Daily Self-Reflection

At the start or end of each day, take a few minutes to reflect on your actions and thoughts. Ask yourself: Did I give away my power today? Did I let other people's opinions or judgments influence my decisions? Journaling can be a helpful tool to track your progress and reinforce your commitment to letting go of the need for external validation.

Set Clear Boundaries Every Day

Whether it's at work, in relationships, or in social situations, make a conscious effort to set boundaries each day. Let people know when you need space, when you're unavailable, or when you're simply not willing to take on extra tasks. Setting these boundaries ensures that you stay focused on your needs and goals without compromising your well-being.

Engage in Mindfulness Practices

Mindfulness techniques—such as meditation, deep breathing, or yoga—can help you stay grounded in the present moment. These practices reduce stress, improve focus, and increase your ability to let go of distractions or negative thoughts that may arise during the day.

Visualize Your Ideal Life

Each morning, take a few moments to visualize your ideal life—the life that reflects your true values and desires. See yourself living free from the pressures of others and taking confident, empowered steps toward your goals. Visualization reinforces your commitment to living authentically and staying true to your own path.

Celebrate Your Wins, Big or Small

At the end of each day, take time to celebrate your wins, whether big or small. This reinforces the importance of internal validation and reminds you that success isn't measured by the opinions of others—it's measured by your ability to stay true to your goals and values.

By incorporating these practices into your daily life, you'll find that the power of Letting Them becomes a natural, effortless part of your mindset. You'll stop worrying about what others think, reclaim your energy and focus, and align your actions with what truly matters to you.

A New Beginning

The Lasting Impact of Letting Go

Throughout this book, we've explored the **power of letting go**—letting go of other people's opinions, the need for external validation, the pressure to control everything, and the limiting beliefs that keep us stuck. But at the heart of the Let Them Theory is something far deeper: **the freedom to live life on your own terms**.

When you begin to let go, you make room for transformation. You release the unnecessary baggage of fear, self-doubt, and societal expectations, and in doing so, you clear the path for personal growth, joy, and fulfillment. This is not just a temporary change; it's a **lasting shift** in how you approach life.

The Let Them Theory offers a timeless framework for living authentically. By consistently choosing to focus on what you can control—your thoughts, your actions, and your energy—you can break free from the cycle of stress and distraction. You are no longer beholden to the opinions of others, nor do you need to prove your worth to anyone. You are free to live with purpose and clarity.

This sense of freedom isn't just theoretical. It's grounded in **real-life results**, as we've seen in the stories shared throughout this book. People who have embraced the Let

Them Theory report feeling more in control of their lives, experiencing less stress, and creating deeper connections with themselves and others.

Letting go doesn't mean giving up or being passive. On the contrary, it's about **actively choosing what to care about** and **aligning your actions with what truly matters** to you. It's about living a life that is authentic, unapologetic, and fully yours.

A Call to Take Action and Embrace Freedom

Now, it's your turn to embrace the freedom that comes with letting go. The Let Them Theory is a call to action—a **bold invitation** to take control of your life, to prioritize yourself, and to start living in alignment with your true desires. It's an opportunity to **shift from living reactively to living proactively**—focusing on the things that truly matter to you, rather than what you feel you "should" do to meet others' expectations.

Take action today by implementing the practices you've learned in this book. It's time to stop waiting for permission from others or for external circumstances to change. Your life, your happiness, and your success are in your hands. Here are some steps to get started:

1. **Reflect on What You Need to Let Go Of** Identify areas in your life where you're holding on

too tightly—whether it's people's expectations, perfectionism, or fear of failure. What's draining your energy and preventing you from moving forward? Make a conscious decision to release these things.

2. **Set Intentions for What You Want to Focus On** Think about what truly matters to you. What are your core values, passions, and goals? Set clear intentions around what you want to prioritize in your life. This will help guide your actions and ensure that you're spending your time and energy on the things that bring you joy and fulfillment.

3. **Create Boundaries to Protect Your Energy** Letting go requires you to set boundaries—whether it's saying no to requests that don't align with your goals or distancing yourself from toxic relationships. Establish healthy limits and communicate them with confidence.

4. **Embrace Imperfection and Celebrate Progress** Letting go of perfectionism is key to moving forward. Remember, progress is more important than perfection. Celebrate every small victory along the way, whether it's building a new habit, creating a boundary, or simply choosing to focus on what brings you peace.

5. **Stay Committed to the Process** Letting go is a practice, not a one-time event. It

takes time and patience to shift your mindset and build new habits. Be gentle with yourself during this process, and stay committed to the path of freedom, self-validation, and personal empowerment.

By taking these steps, you are actively choosing to embrace freedom in your life. You are choosing to let go of the things that don't serve you and to make space for what truly matters. The impact of this decision will be profound—it will create **lasting change** that ripples through every area of your life, from your relationships to your career, to your personal well-being.

This is your new beginning. With the Let Them Theory as your guide, you have everything you need to create a life of joy, fulfillment, and true success. So go ahead, take that first step. Let them go—and let yourself be free.

Made in the USA
Columbia, SC
10 December 2024

48868571R00052